GHOST HOUR

ALSO BY LAURA CRONK
Having Been an Accomplice

Ghost Hour
Poems
Laura Cronk

A Karen & Michael Braziller Book
Persea Books / New York

Persea Books, Inc.
90 Broad Street
New York, New York 10004

Library of Congress Cataloging-in-Publication Data

Names: Cronk, Laura, 1977– author.
Title: Ghost hour : poems / Laura Cronk.
Description: First. | New York : Persea Books, [2020] | "A Karen & Michael Braziller Book." | Summary: "Sometimes compact, sometimes expansive, the poems in Ghost Hour emanate from adolescence and other liminal spaces, considering girlhood and contemporary womanhood-the ways both are fraught with the pleasures and limits of embodiment. As in her previous poetry, Laura Cronk writes personally, intimately, yet never without profound consideration of onslaught of contemporary violence, which we must love in spite of and rage against"—Provided by publisher.
Identifiers: LCCN 2020036194 | ISBN 9780892555192 (paperback)
Subjects: LCGFT: Poetry.
Classification: LCC PS3603.R664 G46 2020 | DDC 811/.6—dc23
LC record available at https://lccn.loc.gov/2020036194

Book design and composition by Rita Lascaro
Typeset in Janson
Manufactured in the United States of America. Printed on acid-free paper

ACKNOWLEDGMENTS

Thank you to the editors of the following journals where some of these poems first appeared, sometimes in earlier forms: *Big Other*, *The Literary Review*, *The Mississippi Review*, *Poem-a-Day*, *The Seventh Wave* and *Stat-O-Rec*. Thank you to Major Jackson who selected "Like a Cat" for *Best American Poetry, 2019*.

Much gratitude to Gabriel Fried, Michael Braziller and Karen Braziller and everyone at Persea Books.

Thank you to my writing community at The New School including early readers Luis Jaramillo, Lori Lynn Turner. Also the wider PPT circle Lisa Freedman, Ben Fama, Leah Iannone, Justin Sherwood, Roberto Montes, Kathryn Squilla, Ricky Tucker, John Reed, and Nicole Drayton. Thanks for continued inspiration to Honor Moore, Robert Polito, David Lehman, and the brilliant faculty and students of the Creative Writing Program.

Thank you for invaluable insight to Gwen Feldman and Gerti Shoen. Thank you to Ashley Malone.

Thank you to Bob Schneider and his Poetry Machine, Geoffrey Nutter and Wallson Glass, Joanna Penn Cooper and her generative flash mob, Colleen Kinder and Owen Murray and The Millay Colony for creating the conditions that allowed many of these poems to be written.

Thank you to Megin Jiménez, sister in poetry, for astute feedback and sustaining friendship. A poem is a poem if you say it is. This book would not be possible without you. Thank you to Jen Mediano for sharing deadlines and passion for making authentic work. Thank you to Matthew Yeager, Wende Crow, and Michael Quattrone and the writing friends I have shared work with over the writing of this book. I am grateful to poetry for bringing so many dear people closer.

Thank you to Duncan Avenue friends in Jersey City. The beauty and hardship of life in a city haunted me during the writing of many of these poems and I'm grateful to have shared the experience with you.

Thank you to my beloved parents and brother and my precious extended family. I will always be grateful for the luck of being born into a family that values art and expression. Thank you also to The Wilson family for their love and support. Thank you to the arts community of my hometown, New Castle, Indiana. I'm thinking now of Richard Willis, cherished teacher whose spirit lives on in the work of his students. Thank you to the friends who shared adolescence with me and inspired some of these poems. "Witching Hour" is for Jeremy Culbertson and Beth Culbertson-Smitherman. "As Made" is for Michael Dudley.

Thank you to Dave, Juliet, and Paul for making this life together so vibrant and full of love.

CONTENTS

I

Ancestry

I never know who is looking
out from my eyes: sadistic German
Catholic or silent Appalachian clockmaker.

The sky is so blue today as I drag the neighbor
boy to the bus, the onion farmer in me
against the army vet in him. There's the

army vet in me, too. He gets things done,
like taking my daughter and the neighbor
boys to the bus, even if one is having a tantrum.

The older children are on the bus and I take
the baby inside. There's the opera singer in him
and the opera singer in me, failed, both of us.

There's the gossip columnist. The one who wore
furs and Shalimar. And the dairy farmers.
There's the poet who had séances, and the dead

who talked and talked to everyone but her.
She is glad to be playing on the floor with the baby,
glad to come with me to the kitchen

to cook him eggs. There are the small-game hunters.
Banjo pickers. Football coach. The general manager
of the factory and the factory line man are both here,

looking into my mirror as I pin my hair and
put on earrings. There's the hairdresser. There are
the twins. Both were painters and stopped at the

same time, when one of them died. There's the other pair
of twins, alto and soprano. They are arguing about my outfit,
but I don't have time to change. I just have to go.

I put on my coat, say goodbye to my son
and the neighbor who came over to watch him.
The onion farmer's vicious wife is putting on my gloves.

There are the ones who played ice hockey but they're not
helping. It's so cold. This unending winter might break me.
Now I'm inhabited by a whole group of the good-for-nothing

ones, with their side-long looks and wispy hair,
delicate, who never made their mark or even had a trade.
Everyday we leave together. They walk me to the train.

Before

I was exquisitely thin, having just mowed the yard. I was hungry, but put off eating to lie in the grass by the paddle-boat dock. The summer feeling I want to pay for. There were wildflowers exploding behind the aluminum fence. There were rocks so smooth from the water, no that was you. I was so young that I did calisthenics every night to be ready for what had to come my way. I was so broke that I changed into my bandana skirt in the employee bathroom. We had nothing to do but break into the golf course at night and know nothing about the constellations. When I saw you, high in the supermarket, two summers after moving away, we had nothing to say. I was so young that I brought the boxer who sat in my station after his dish-washing shift a glass of milk. He ate Beef Manhattan, green beans, and a piece of peanut butter pie. He was you. I was so thin that I never ate the lunch special. I could have leapt from the railing of my father's porch. I had no sense of my body's limitations. I did and we lie side by side on the golf course talking about how a person didn't need to go to college. We were so young and you had just shorn your white blond curls. We were so broke and we didn't touch, except I ran my hand across your scalp sometimes. I was walking from the parking lot of the foundry to the foundry office to see if they had filing jobs, you came out and said, *What are you doing here? Turn around.* Later you said, *But this is home.* We were so young, so broke, existing on a thin, faint hit of life, amid the over-fertilized bean fields and half-closed factories and wet asphalt, the vapor that was me and the vapor that was you.

White

My children are white.
I'm just as white.
Writing it I'm not less white.

When she was born I said,
She is so beautiful. He said,
She looks like a white baby.
She looks, white.

As kids
we thought we could
stop using aerosol

hairspray. We thought
we could go on
eating sno-cones,

tanning in the yard,
pulling our straps to see
our tan lines, white.

But the white people
left the lights on
all night. Every night.

Burned up everything.
Burned through what's
underground and dug

deeper. Burned up the sky.
Burned through brightness
into brightness, leaving holes.

The sun says, *I see you,*
each and every white
one of you. I see you—
cancerous, half-blind, white.

Mixed Class

The kids who volunteered
for the crisis hotline

did it for a reason.
We wanted to help

ourselves.
Needed to hear

other people's confessions.
 We were all the same—

the marching band dorks,
the crisis hotline kids,

the academic
quiz-bowl geeks—

We did well in school
and wore off-brand jeans

and off-brand shoes.
We went to church lock-ins

and were saved, buzzing
with soda.

We took the bus to
symphonies and museums.

When we got home, one
of us walked in to find

fake plastic shit
on a plate in the fridge.

We memorized lines
for the summer play.

Gay or in love
with someone who was gay.

We worked at the gas station,
or Hardees, mowed grass.

Went to the country club
but just to the Coke machine.

From the high-class side,
one mom said

she was leaving dad
for artistic reasons.

Really, it was
alcoholic devastation

from the
previous generation.

A reason to sign up
to do the play

was to have someone else's
words to say.

From Amanda's mom,
a quote, not so sweet,

Now you can't say there's not
shit to eat.

Before

If the idea of folding and unfolding comes
from the flower, the flower drawing water
from the ground and opening it into the air,
and if my boyfriend when I was nineteen said
that his mom said that the foot draws energy
from the ground beneath and that our
modern problems come from wearing shoes,
then what?

His thyroid was crushed when she
ran over him in her car when he was three,
or someone else ran over him and she was
too high to help? I believed that when he told me,
though I knew he lied, or else left things out.
A new leaf with the edge bitten or ripped.
His skin was so smooth it was beyond all sense,
which is the other thing I remember.

Yellow Wild Flower

I can eat as much as a big man. Wiry stems scarf up
sunlight, roots muscle through dirt getting at water.
If I could walk, I would run. Instead I shoot up
starburst buds and pinwheels of thick yellow.
Behind each bloom that's going white at the edges,
about to look nibbled or crumpled or done,
there's another spikey ball, ready. If I could walk,
I would never sit down. I stand straight, pixie cut
ruffled in the wind. There's no swaying, there's no
lolling a lush peony head toward all I want, hinting
hard. If I'm hungry, I say it. I eat and grow. I dare you
to scan this meadow and tell me you're not thinking
yellow, yellow, yellow.

Witching Hour

The dirt and grass
and maple trees and scrub trees
and day lilies and clover
and the dew
that bathes them

and the clay
beneath the dirt
and the water
beneath the clay—

On deep summer nights,
these elements,
in counsel with each other
decide to share
their power with the children.

Children still entangled
with plants and dirt,
capable of finding
hundreds
of places to hide.

And before
the children
break out of childhood,
but just before,
at the peak
of their own natural power,
the dirt and the plants
and the darkness
send the parents
to bed.

The children will be out
with flashlights
hiding from each other
and finding each other.

They meet
in the back
of the Culbertson's house,
which has the biggest yard.
It spans behind
their house, beside
their industrial garage,
across the old sawmill alley,
to a barn and dog cages,
and farther
to a dirt bike track
marking the edge of a field.

The children decide
which one will stand
by the tallest maple alone
in the circle of light
from the garage flood lamp
and cover his eyes
and count.

One of the girls flies
over the grass
in the blackness.
She scrapes the low branches,
keeps running
and flings herself
to the wet grass

behind a short rise
marked with a stone.

There's a boy
already there.
Mid dive when she
realized, it was too
late to find another spot.

They say nothing and watch
and feel with their breath
and hearing and sight
that has changed
into a sense
they carry as an aura
and can be cast
around them in the dark
two feet on all sides.

Time passes in the quiet
of their breathing and
the sounds of nearby crickets
and bats sweeping overhead.

Their eyes adjust and
they look at each other's
faces in the dimmest blue.

In the dark, the boy's face
is like a river rock.
There is one small streak
of dirt at the top
of his sharp cheekbone

and all of his skin
gleams with sweat.
The girl wants
to keep looking,
doesn't want to be found.

And before
the dirt and the plants
notice and after the boy
with the flashlight
finds them
but before the
other children
are called out,
the girl asks
and orders
all at once,
again. Again!

Ancestry

If the quiet Appalachian clock maker,
If his friends. If their pastor
and their wives. If his wife.
If it didn't need to be hidden.
If the clockmaker.

I resisted knowing.

It's true even though.
If he was the gentle one.
If his children.
If he held them easily.
If his rough hand smoothed their hair.
If, before he left, he tossed
them in the air.

If the twins, with their
two minds
sensed something impure.
If they didn't.

If his shirt was freshly pressed.
If his shoes were shined.
If he only had
one pair of shoes.

If his walking down
the steps and onto the street
and gathering with the others.
If flowing toward the church basement.

If changing there,
putting on hoods and robes.
If the town turned out.
If they clapped and
cheered and ate sweets.

If he marched with the others
ghostly but unbothered.
If everyone there, unhooded,
in plain sight,
was unbothered too.
If they all knew anyway who
each man in each hood
was by his shoes.

If that's where I'm from
and who.

If what was taught at school
was dismissed outside.
If the chasm was just
left there open
and like other adult things
made no sense.

If my grandfather,
the kind one, the gentle one.

If he marched. If he didn't
disagree. If his thoughts
were the rope and the tree.
If I was raised to protect
the rope and the tree.

Before

The neighbors didn't say much
and we didn't say much.
The baked dirt of August
communicated nothing.
The dog rarely barked.
The horses just looked.
The pine tree waved when
there was heavy wind
but mostly stood
silent, but for the slip
of needles from branches,
the taffeta whoosh of them
as we passed around
the side of the house.
Our parents didn't fit—
they answered our questions
when we asked. Our
mother took it
further and went with
her guitar outside
to sit and play
on the concrete steps
hoping someone would
happen by and hear.

Our friends' parents

weren't like that.

Our friends weren't.

Teachers said

what was needed.

First loves didn't know

what to say.

The vast fields were silent

when you stood at the edge.

If you climbed over the locked

gate and walked out

into the rows of beans you

could hear the rustling of

the dry pods and the clicks

of insects that hadn't

been killed by spray.

There was something

else here before

but we didn't talk about

what it meant

or what it was or who.

Dear Autobiography

You had a knack for making a home wherever you were. I
benefited from that. You hung dried flowers from the window
latch, taped up cutout art on the wall. The small pieces of pottery
you'd made, your bag with needles and yarn. You brought the
stereo and the CDs. Your desk was beautifully arranged. Mine
was a pile of things propped on legs, papers, half considered
whatevers. I hadn't yet read the books that would teach me
to deal with the objects in life, one by one. I must have been
maddening to live with. Your head of gorgeous curls. The small
brown sweater you knitted. We were so often in the dark or in
candle light. I had a vision of living in a round adobe house on a
path far from everything, except you. We loved each other and
we loved the same boy and he loved us and another girl we didn't
know well except to know she was somehow our opposite, each
of us. I'm on the train now, holding this paper in my forty-year
old hands, watching the backs of buildings flash by in the dark. It
was so confusing then to have just broken out of the chrysalis of
childhood, to be in our adult bodies, knowing nothing, lesbian folk
emanating from our small room, our hands in each other's hair.

The cat on the bed was a beautiful thing we had. Rooms with furniture and carpet. We had our children's sized pajamas. We had eaten dinner. We were a brother and sister with a cat sitting between us. What are we doing to do? There was nothing we could do. When I try to look at the girl I was then, it's harder because she was without a body. She had watched her father leave that afternoon with one laundry basket of clothes. Seeing him have to go made her own body evaporate. Was this how the ghost that lived in the upstairs closet felt? Evaporated? She stood by her parents' bedroom door the last morning he woke there and heard him crying, a sound she didn't know. She had no legs to bring her into the room, no arms to wrap around him. She sat with her brother, the bedside lamp making a circle of light they perched at the edges of. He had become a little boy ghost. Their father in his car driving and driving had to become one too.

The night when we were on our way back from something, I'll let myself think of it. We were walking back from studying. Or maybe it was a reading or a play? You led us off the sidewalk and we began to study the trees, the black canopy they made over us, their stark shapes against the wet haze of dark sky. The campus receded, the sidewalk did, we were there in the humid air on earth that churned death and life together in thousand year old clumps. You dropped your bag and stood very still. The trees creaked and moaned, breathing. I heard my own breathing, felt my heart beating. You closed your eyes. You went on to marry a dancer and not the other girl you loved or the girl we both loved or me. You lifted up your arms slowly. I knew what you were doing and you knew I would know. I walked over close and inspected you. Fellow French horn player, new friend, cute in overalls and your hair cut blunt. There were your arms overhead, your face upturned, that unlined face a perfect leaf. You married someone who knows our bodies are more than anyone tells us they are. I dropped my bag and found a treeless spot on the soft ground and lifted up my arms too. How long did we spend in that grove? New fall air on our limbs. We hadn't kissed yet. The shape you made in silhouette. The trees became boyish and girlish and we became trees.

Because the idea of a choice itself is so positive. Because I like offering choices. It's pleasurable being a hostess with myriad offerings on platters, prepped for eager fingers to pluck. Because I read the cheeky what wave feminist destigmatizing think pieces. Because I am a feminist. Because when an aunt told me about her experience I said I'm pro-choice too. Because she said, really? So unlike her, like a little girl. Because I didn't trust the flash of feeling I had, it's a boy, that sense of instant knowing. Because I couldn't have anticipated calling out of work and making my way to St. John the Divine and finding an empty chapel there with a light blue ceiling and stars, the heaven I decided my little boy was swimming in. Because the candles I lit and light. Because I prayed to the God I can't make a decision about and asked him? her? it? to take care of my boy. Because I didn't know until it was too late that it was a spiritual choice for me and not political. Because my politics are unchanged. Because the day was gray and empty and raining and cold and stupid. In the numerology of my life, something somewhere made a choice for me about the 17th day of whatever month gods or men decided to organize days and lives into.

Where I'm at is a place of quick fixes and workarounds. It's my hyper local cuisine. Where I'm at is rich in hasty dinners, children's arms flung across my sleeping face, a steady job with a ride on a commuter train. Tonight on the train, the man next to me sighed as I sat down, dramatically re-arranged his bags. I didn't waver. The conductor huffed when I forgot to have my ticket ready. I regularly bother people and they bother me and it's simple, this annoyed sibling state of being on the train. Tonight I pulled out my notebook and tried to write, looking straight ahead at the burgundy pleather of the bench seats, patched with burgundy duct tape, two bald spots on two heads jostling in unison above. As I took notes on the bald spots, the man next to me looked plainly into my lap trying to read as I wrote. I looked just past him, out into the black distance of the window, willing him to stop. He stopped. Where I'm at is that I only read and write on the train. I give myself this time when I'm officially nowhere. Where I'm at is finding what's possible without effort that anyone else could ever see. And now in the marathon evening hours of getting a family to bed I'm out of hiding, typing, my son on my lap. He's going to add the final punctuation.

II

As Made

We were made
         for each other.

God gave

/ a little shrug.

Star-crossed,
         crossed again,

double   crossed.

The black   galaxy   touched
         clumps of dirt—

         creaking
                    there.

This is my story   of our story.
              It reaches back into time.

What part of us still knows

              how the stars   pinned us   how

              the night sky held us
                    after each lifetime

before swirling us up again,

sending us back
into this?

Morning wedding / past lives.

Instead of a veil,
a blindfold

or hood.

On one day
of each generation

going back

endlessly

we married.

The wedding was in

the Methodist church,

the Baptist   church,

the Catholic   church,

my mother's   living room.

I wore

      a Sunday dress,   a

      cotton   sheath   with sash,   a

      powder blue suit,   a

            white   satin dress.
             Pins   left in.

You wore a dark suit

      each time.

We slept

      on a bed of gravel,

                     glass,

             sticks,
    nails.

A poem
        is private.
    No one
          reads
          a poem

but   someone

in trouble.

***

We were   in trouble.

Are we
in trouble now?

Raised in the same   place,

with   the same manners,

and there was

(what was it)

something else.

We met at twelve.

Two kids who seemed

the least in trouble

of any kids anyone knew.

I recognized   you.

***

It doesn't   matter
        what play it was.

                Just that
        there was a backstage—

we met   in that   good dream.

I closed the doors   of
                the family car,

                crossed
        the school parking   lot,
                and walked right into it.

There you were,
maybe your dad
                was measuring   wood
                        for the set.

        Maybe my mom
was flirting   with the director.

They were near,   but we were far away.

        The place between
                imagination

                and waking life

                        that was familiar.

33

It was a whole world   in darkness.

     Pools of light   buzzing,
          against the wood and concrete
           and mirrors of backstage,

     street lamps
         for an underworld, otherworld—

a place where there's friendship
     but no street clothes,

       where there's work
to be done in the dark.

That art existed where we were,
         small industrial town,
     island   in a sea   of bean fields and corn fields,
communal art
     at that,

meant there was some kind of God

who loved us
and knew us.

    ***

I went to the Catholic church.

     You went to   the Church of God.

My church was so   opaque,

If anyone there felt anything   they kept it quiet.

I liked getting to sing,
        speak all at once   with the others
                in a kind of poetry.   I liked

the stained glass,   the papery yeast   of the wafer,

        the smell of the wafer   on my mother's breath.

I liked the sip of water mixed   with sweet wine,

        the faint smell of incense.   I liked the priest saying one thing
                had instantly become another.   I liked
the art in it.

The art of your church seemed   simple,
                unworthy of you.

                Did you try   not to judge

        the language that seemed   bought
                at Kmart, the upbeat
                        music?

                Did you enjoy the cheerfulness?

The Catholics were humorless
        but at least   there was privacy.

I know that you, though,   were expected

to let Jesus

all the way into your heart.

I saw a Young Life brochure   showing how.

Plan a night   you could be alone,

schedule a kind of date with him.

Make a meal and
set two places.

There was a cartoon drawing
of a teenaged   boy with food set out

for two
and a hazy,   handsome man
in robes
half-sketched   across.

It wasn't supposed to be symbolic.   It was an exercise
like poets devise.   He was really supposed to show
if you believed.

I never asked you what you thought
of the expectation that you   get so close

with this muse,   half guy half god,
who seemed great,

but who was also supposed to be
your most judgy friend.

Did you
let him into your heart?

What did he do there?

***

We were friends
and our friends   were all friends

You were funny   and nerdy and
athletic and cute.

We went bowling,   went to the movies.
We joined everything   all together,

not just community theater   but science club,
the speech team,   youth groups,
marching band.
We learned
crisis mediation   and agreed
to be called to the office
if anyone   was in trouble.

Surely the last thing   kids publicly in trouble

would want   is another kid
there to "mediate"

but we were ready to help,
                              ready to work.
          Anything dorky,   artistic,   spiritual,
                    or altruistic
          had a roster with
our names on it.

My name was there   and yours,
          alphabetically,
just after mine.

   ***

Our young selves   are gone, as much
          as anyone or anything

                    that has ever lived is gone.

Which is to say   never over.

   ***

We went on dates as friends   and then

          as chaste-est boyfriend/girlfriend.

                    We watched Legends of the Fall
                         at the Castle theater.

          I couldn't pull myself   together at the end.
Teenaged feelings   unleashed at the tragic final scene.

And you know the electricity   of two people
          sitting together   in a theater   who haven't
                    yet really touched?   There was some of that

                    but the fizzing and sparks
                                        not between   you and me,
                    but between you and me and
                                        gorgeous, young
                                        Brad Pitt,
          moody and doomed
                    in a landscape
                                        we recognized.

We were made of
                    bits of   opal,   corn silk,

                    malachite,   cave mud,
          the wine red   interior fabric

of an old Chevet.

You worked harder   than me.
                    You wanted   to be taken seriously.

          You wanted children, a career.
                    You wanted   a dignified life.

I wanted   to do   well enough
          to be put in the   smart kid classes,
where the conversations were good.

Before a camping trip
        to the Canadian Rockies
        you asked me   to be your girlfriend.

                You were going to be gone
        almost all summer.   We met

                on my porch early.
                Everything cool and fresh.

Your class ring,   compact piece   of steel,
        so smooth   on the inside, set with
                an emerald.   I think there was
        an awkward kiss.

I wrapped string around it
        taped the string   so it would stay on my finger.
                Teenage ceremony

                        that didn't fit.

                You sent postcards   packed with writing
                Funny pictures—   one of just flat blackness
                        "The Badlands at Night"

                Another was an old movie still,
                Canadian Mounties standing all in a line
kissing their horses.

Is it a kind of queerness,
                loving someone queer?

No.   But what is it?

What is mine

                    and isn't   mine
to confess?

We had to cycle   through something.
            We had lived
                    so many lives together.

        We were and weren't   were and weren't.

        We were sitting together
                on the band bus   scrunched low in the seats
                        resting our heads
        against each other. We were holding hands on hay rides

        and then we weren't.

                This is my story
                            of our story
                    of being young.

And the disaster we averted.

There was Mary Todd and
            Abraham, Franklin and

Eleanor, and

I wanted you to lie, your parents wanted you to lie, your
church wanted you to lie.

There was a friend you had from the swim team.

Did you appreciate, as I did,   when I sat behind him
in math class   his strong, tanned legs,

the clean syllables of his name   and the way he smiled so easily
and hardly spoke?

You both smelled   like chlorine all the time.

You went hunting together.
Your parents helped you   roast the squirrels
you brought back.

Even though we lived   where we lived,
it was a novelty.   We were a generation out

from the real   squirrel hunters.   But you got to be

out in the woods   with a beautiful
quiet boy,   there was that.

Am I getting any of this right?

You tried to come out to me.   I couldn't hear.
I could see though.

The way you changed   in front of Ben,
when he had just moved to town.

42

He was the first person

any of us met who was   undeniably,
             who just—

    He was homeschooled,

    from a conservative Christian family,
    soft-spoken and lovely.   And odd.

    Odd because of being homeschooled?

You didn't think   he was odd at all.

    When he was near   your face softened,
    you oriented yourself toward him,
        a plant in the presence of sun.

Am I getting any of this   right at all?

To get it wrong. We're both alive, but this is an elegy and
       getting any kind of elegy wrong—

    what is worse than that?

Senior year   marching band.
    White and Kelly green military uniforms,

      hats with plumes. We were serious.

Our teacher chose esoteric, experimental music
like we were a professional   drum corps,

      not a pep band.

      You were drum major.   It was the year
           the show opened
with a French horn solo.

      (French horn solo!)

In the blind audition, Amanda and I
     played   over and over.

We stood shaking,   reassuring each other.

Each time our teacher said *Again!*
I pictured the notes lifting and flying,

      imagined their shapes
         as they flew across   the humid football field.

      I wasn't the most exact
        but I got the tone.

The other thing was you. I was sending the notes to you.

I got the part   and every rehearsal and every show

began with the two of us.   You looked at me
   and held out your hands   *Now.*

I sent the most perfect,
mournful notes I could.   *Here.*

We were cast as Elizabeth   and John Proctor
in the fall play.

Probably at least somewhat   believable
as a long-married couple

tormented by a secret
and misguided neighbors.

There was the feeling   of impossible love.
There was love,   but

it wasn't possible.

I found out   you carved
in your desk
your freshman year   at college
in Latin

"It's not my fault"

I can imagine   you learning

a whole dead language
to be able to write
just that.

I'm holding   my   girlhood
          in my hands.

          I see your face   as it was   then.

                    Cute and queer
                              and perfect.

                    You saved us.
                    I never told you

                    that I was grateful.

We are   what's

          written
                    in the dust

on the hood
          of the old Chevet.

One night   I heard voices
          as I sat alone
                    in my room.   I opened

                    the window,   looked out.

                              The black sky

was overfull with stars,

so studded   with stars

some might fall out.

There was a security light

on a pole where our yard

met a field.

I looked down.

It was you.

You came to sing to me,

with another boy,
in your hunting boots.

III

What to Eat

The way to be a powerful
forty-year-old woman
is not to eat.

The way to be a powerful
fifty-year-old woman
is to order sparkling water.

The way to be a powerful
forty-five-year-old woman
is to cross your arms
and stand back
when the birthday cake
is passed.

To be incredibly
powerful at twenty—
don't eat.

At thirty, it helps
not to eat.

At sixty you can be
powerful not eating.

A seventy-year-old
Italian countess orders
only steamed vegetables
and has a fifty-year-old wife.

Actresses interviewed
for magazine profiles
order steak frites, chowder,
beer, pieces of pie and coffee,
but we know they don't eat.

A man, a famous actor
in his fifties, sat with
a journalist at his own
coffee table.

He blinked back
a headache and ate
chopped salad with
oil free vinaigrette.
His decorative girlfriend
wandered past.

To be powerful and artistic
and a man—
it is good not to eat.

What to eat: almonds soaked
in water for twenty minutes,
rice milk, avocado, fish.

I can see the wonderful things
that would happen for me
if I would not eat.

Just like my sister.
She locked herself
in her room and stayed there
for months.

She had her baby,
gave it away,
and went back
to her room.

She ate only boiled
chicken and apples.
She emerged thin

with just enough suffering
legible on her face
to make her truly beautiful.

Thirst

Unclouded third eye
and lush red wings.
I'm pouring water
from cup to cup.
This is the water
we are meant to drink
with the other animals.
There are daffodils
by the water, a road
leading from the water
to the shining crown
of the sun. My white
hospital gown—
off-the-rack
and totally sane.
My foot unsteady
though, heel held
aloft, missing its stiletto.

Nine months sober
emblazoned
on my flat chest
in red below girlish
curls and mannish chin.
You can't see my eyes.
You've never seen them.

Rest

I wish I was a priest.
I wish I wore buffalo horns
and an ivory orb
as a miter on my head.
High holidays and times
of despair—
what to do
and more importantly
what to wear
decided,
unyieldingly glam,
form untraceable
beneath the pooling blue.
I wish I had that far off look,
holding up a white flag
to the crazed fertility
coming between me
and the great, pure ocean.

Dusk

The moment when everything
has to be finished
or abandoned.

It can never be finished.
So, abandoned.

Everyday, how to quit the day,
walk out.

The light.
It gets sharper
before it gets darker.

Look, the shoes
I wore when I was ten
are on my feet again,

glowing white.
The trees saved up
their color all day

and are throwing it off
while the sky goes gray.

A truckload of yearning
is dropped at my door
each dusk.

The shipment
stacked sharp against
the pink silk sky.

It's night's work
to prepare it, arrange it,
clean it, cook it.

Or,
blurry,
slip into it.

*

I just want to be pushed
against a wall and kissed
by a drink,

held at the swerving
tip of a green stem.

If pleasure wastes,
uses up,

the thread, unspooled
unable to quite spool again,

I don't care. I want
to be unspooled
by a drink.

I want the dimmer
switch pressed and turned.

I want the incandescent
light, I want
the privacy of a drink.

I want to pick the meat off
the bone, drag it through
salt, alone.

I want
the taste of oblivion.

In the ghost hour
when everything
that's lost

or gone
is really gone,

I want a drink.

The Cat Session

My session started right on time. I was terrified but you were my
guide and I trusted you. If it turned out to be a joke, it would be
a good joke. If it turned out to do what was promised, it would
save me. The skyline glimmered below us where we sat in your
apartment on the 39th floor. This was a part of the treatment,
feeling untouchably wealthy, if just for an hour. Everything was
behind me as I sat on your modern Italian sofa: the shitty Monday
mood I'd carried in; the speculative thoughts I had that were
doing me no good. The nightmare square at the center of my
chest was the reason I came, maybe even that could lose its hold
over me. I was starting to feel vulnerable and close to something
real. It was not appropriate to ask but this was new territory.
Won't you hold me, I wondered half-way through the session. *No,*
you said. *Keep petting the cat.* A solid gray one was resting next to
me just then. Your beard was sexy in the dusk and surely smelled
good, I stared at it and kept petting. I realized the cat session was
going all wrong. As the cats roamed the penthouse and as I tried
to give myself over to their healing energy, I became more stiff
and cold, nearly inanimate, the nightmare the only thing about
me that was alive. The nightmare was throbbing and hot, growing
in strength. The cats knew, but ignored it. Their indifference was
supposed to help, but I had perceptive, cold people peppering my
life already. The cats added a new dimension to my torment. *I
won't be back*, I said, slipping you my co-pay, tears running down
my face. *But the cat sessions build on each other,* you said, *I think you
had a breakthrough; this is just the beginning.* I knew that more
sessions would only mean more pain. However beautiful the pain,
high above the city and surrounded by lustrous cats, I couldn't
bear it.

Today: What is Sexy

Construction worker
with two long French braids,
sexy.

Woman in high-waisted
jeans, white t-shirt,
plain sandals,
sexy.

City sidewalks,
in general.

Breeze,
warm.

Rainbow heart
Pride sticker
on the sidewalk,
sexy.

Having the door
held at coffee shop.

Tiny portions of food
at the coffee shop,
sexy.

The restraint
cancelling out the lack
of generosity.

The iron gate
around
the dry cleaner's,
sexy.

The black glossy paint,
tipped with fussy,
thornish fleur-de-lis.

The pot of periwinkle
hydrangeas,

huge haphazard
balls of blooms,
sexy.

Woman with gray hair,
tangerine shorts, tan legs,
jay-walking,
sexy.

Two people walking
ahead of me in culottes.

The impulse to react
against skinny jeans.

Dizzy in
the revolving door.

Ducking into the
open green room
to put on mascara.

Green room in low light.
Someone practicing piano
on a dark stage.

Building that holds
the ghosts of dances
choreographed

in basement studios,
sexy.

Suites of offices
on the upper floors,
not.

Stepping into
a crowded
elevator,
no.

And finally,
arriving
at my desk.

That's not
sexy.

But the view

from the window—

the Forbidden River,

calling.

To My Twenties

Stop what you're doing
and come with me. We'll
walk out into the wild
cold, you in your pink
sequined shell from the
consignment shop –
you can have my coat.
Let's be out together
in the world, the wind
beating against us, the
sidewalks cracking with
ice. Though you shrink
from the cold, my twenties,
you're still lustrous, still
throwing off heat. We'll
walk past the schizophrenic
piano player and the junk
dealer poet, there are bad
boyfriends around every
bend, but we're together
now and we don't have
to stop. We'll go back
to my apartment and
open the door and the

kids' faces will pop
with happiness. They'll
run toward us, ram their
heads into our stomachs,
so eager to be held.
It's not the kind of
greeting you're used to.
After dinner I'll get you
a cab, my twenties,
but you'll take the shape
of a great gray bird
and fly away.

Mythological Rape Painting

I hate this stuff, that the rapist is a god is such a boring
part of the story. The gods are fucking with us, that's
the moral? Our hands in the air as we're grabbed
from behind. No one rides a horse in the nude, and still,
it's not an invitation. I don't want to look at the fat half orbs
 of our breasts trying to leap out of the scene, our voluminous
hair flying behind and whipping together with Zeus's
aggressive curls. The horse has a horn, which really, we get it.
Our faces held to the canvases of rape paintings
in museums all over the world. We wouldn't have missed it
anyway, our destiny. Bearing children, demigods, who will
ruin and be ruined by the world in equal measure.

Judgement

He moistens his lips
in the street light
and waits. Or wait,
am I the man? I am.
Asking the price,
setting the time.
Every tank top is frayed
and too tight, summer
too deep to come out
of, every thought
overripe, so sweet
before it reeks. I will use
the two more
years I have of youth
spend-thrift,
waste them, trash them.

But What of Holding the Keys to Freedom

Who called out to me
when my pace slowed?
"Skank," the voice said,

the razor wire
that's around anything
nice shining in the dark.

The thing is, I am a thing walking,
another nothing,
can to be crushed, bone to be gnawed

Cycles

A swirl of trash
I'm dodging it
A gust of nasty wind
Now you're about to be
Even more remote

Look at me, complete bitch
With nowhere to go
Companion
In tan pants
I am what to you?

My people wear sneakers
While they hunt and fish
Short perms, cuntish
So I shouldn't say

That something is
Wrong with you
Because you grew up
In an asshole place

Together we made
Our way here
Where the neighbor's noise
Drives you deeply inside
Where each A in my name
Becomes a long pit, a grave

Where I've got something
In my tooth, some smudge
On my face, something off
Wrong, nothing light now.
Nothing lit up, bright, aflame.

Faith

The smoglike mixture

of spectators and actors

the magician-medic of

the dollar store plus

the chariot driver of the

double-sphinx

jitney bus plus

the rest of us

this place has

an elemental nature

you just can't see it I slip

into primeval bird mode

and try to sense

with my skin and my head

turning side to side what is

the good and what

is the poison

the chromium dump

which building was built over it

the deformed pigeon

on the air conditioner

will it make a nest

and stay

Marriage

Neither nickeled nor dimed
Neither paid nor fined
Neither wined nor dined
Neither free nor rhymed

Neither bird nor vine
Neither leaf nor spine
Neither cruel nor kind
Neither yours nor mine

Weather Poem

Some scientists interpret the light bands and spots as cloud-filled
storms and the dark bands and spots as regions of good weather.
Is your reticenceweather? Static? An inherited light band with
spots of chill? As the scientistssay, "No one really knows." Maybe,
as when we met, all information is rightin front of me. I can't see
it. I'm sending up this balloon borne telescope, launching this
planetary fly-by.

Poem of Attraction

Seduction is not that which is opposed to production. Seduction is that which attracts production. Absence is not that which is opposed to presence, but that which seduces presence. I think it's clear what I'm trying to say. The lightning flash of seduction melts the polar circuits of meaning. Call out to my presence and it will come.

Vegetarian Poem

Now we are only half human being. We do things with hesitation, we do things with ego. Even when we don't hesitate, we do things with ego. Yeah, I know I was vegetarian because the God inside us wants it. But then I quit. Started to buy, cook, eat meat all the time. The God inside me is buried. And doing what? We knew the climate was too hot and wet for us – two reserved types unless drinking and dancing for one, and drinking and drinking for the other – but we came here to taste and spit out the food with the power of God's mercy.

Poem of Chance

You who read this would have never been born. The purely
chance events are as follows: coming to a large tomb at twilight
and finding a ghost there, pointing, stating this is my grave; a
dream of making a kite, which denotes seeking to win the one
you love with misrepresentations; the creation of small square
sheets of cheap paper adorned with pictures or stamped with a
crudely carved die of houses, chairs, carts, horses, implements for
cooking, the toilette, and writing.

Love Poem

The real abbess of this convent just slipped into the parish photo-booth instead of preparing a proper liturgy. The liturgy was a mess, inarticulate gibberish chanted by gardeners wearing rounds of orange peel instead of spectacles, holding their books upside down. I didn't even notice. I was sending the picture to you. You, in pressed shirt, body of pink-edged sulphur, bedstraw hawk-moth, white-lined sphinx, so elemental and beautiful, I'm filled with anger and hunger, in other words love.

Like a Cat

You want a dog
but you are like a cat,
though you hate cats,
which is a very cat-like
position. I want a cat
but you're allergic
so we'll get a dog
who will be like me.
Besides, I realize that,
having you, I already
have a cat. You have
intense fixations, like
a cat. Though you're
tall and strong, you walk
lightly on the balls
of your feet, like a cat.
You're good at
everything you ever
try to do. In your
reticence you'd rather
not be written about or
analyzed, like a cat.
But you are very good
to look at, to study,
in your many moods
and attitudes, like a cat.
And your affection
is sudden and real,
radiating mystery
and heat beside me,
like a cat.

On Choosing You

You brought love letters from other loves,
records of overdraft, furniture found on
the street. You brought unsophisticated
drawings you made in charcoal and that
wasn't enough. You brought pages of
your musings, recordings of your voice.
You realized your mistake and brought
bundles of sheets washed and folded tight,
platters of roast chicken, hand creams,
sweets. You sang and your voice gave out.
You started a fight. You caught my eye
while you were looking mournful. Late
at night, after walking together, you gave me
a single photo of you in the future, very old.
You dreamt you were a fish and told me
about it and I could see it all so clearly.

The Sculptor

I'm sorry I'm not

a sculptor

your profile your

shapely head

I'm thinking deeply

through the feeling

I'm sorry

I'm not

a sculptor

the structure

of you

the tree

you are to climb

I'm sorry I'm not

a sculptor

your inwardness

you wear it

on your lips

the shape

of your lips

makes me want

to be a sculptor

they were the first

true glimpse

of our daughter

I'm sorry I'm

not a sculptor

who but me

knows this

feeling

I'm not fulfilling

my responsibility

I pledged to

love you

and protect you

I can see that

you could be

painted

could be

written

should be

sculpted

we know what

time takes

what if

I could

do more?

Mother Poem

Being a mother
doesn't feel like
being a mother
it feels like
being me
taking a small hand
saying *okay*
let's go.

The Professionals

Who decorates movie sets, sitcom stages,

the kitchens used to advertise paper towels?

Who decorates doctor's offices, the suite

of offices of a university president, of

a Wall Street accounting firm? Who chose

the paint color for the steel doors at

the bus terminal, the window casements

of the post office, who picked out the awning

at the hospital entrance? All of the patients

in the ER waiting room are held in an embrace

of turquoise and beige that was someone's

decision fifteen years ago. The spy in the new

series has art on the walls of her D.C. house.

When did she hang it? A set designer wondered this

while hammering the nails. In the evenings

and on weekends, I make the decisions one by one.

Mid-century with a Victorian nod, Farmhouse

Minimalism, Scavenger Maximalism

with a sense of humor and on a budget.

It's never quite right and never done.

The Shakers hung their chairs on walls.

They shook together but never touched.

Is that how they could do it? Make a home

and live in it, all at once?

Garden of Earthly Delights

A view appears.
I forget, always,
that we are on a hill,
that land is beneath us,
soil, clay, rock.
A view appears
as I leave my block:

a black iron bridge,
water towers,
smokestacks,
an elevated highway.
A moat of awfulness,
a friend said, encircles
Jersey City.
You must go through
the moat getting in
or getting out.

If the 1 & 9, the refineries,
the loading docks, the
contaminated marshes
are the moat, then this
is the castle.

From the roof of
our building
you can see New York.

We move in and out
of each other's apartments—
to borrow something, to talk,
to drink. After a break-up,

a death, a lay-off,
we sit on the steps,
smoking or not,
watching traffic.

We work for each other,
paid and unpaid work,
cleaning, watching kids,
moving heavy things.
We barbecue in the back
and prop open the gate
with traffic cones.

We throw hard-boiled eggs
at the men ripping open
the trash, we rip open the trash,
we sit on the stoop watching.

We eat stone soup, we cook stone
soup, we volunteer for stone
soup clean-up, we knock over
the sign advertising community
stone soup with our strollers and
keep walking.

We do yoga in the backyard
listening to sirens,
cooking sounds, children.

We turn up the radio
as we sit in our car
waiting for each other,
we lean in the

car window as
we're walking by
because we like the song,
we hate when our ride
turns up the music.

We chase a man
down the street
who never cleans up
after his dog. We think
it's stupid to carry little
bags to pick up dog
shit. We hang
gifts for new babies
on each other's doors.

We hang bags of
hand-me-down clothes
outgrown by the biggest
on the doors of the smallest.
We fight in the street
in front of our kids,
we share a cab, we choose
cantaloupes together
at the fruit stand,
we throw things down,
we sweep them up.

We congregate
on a couch
that was put out
for Big Trash Night
under the sycamores

at the curb.
We watch
the children playing
in the bath
of evening air
in this city
of their first memories.

Portrait of The Summer Husband

You said it was like
we were living on a pod
on the sun. Top floor
walkup. You hauled
buckets with soil and seeds
to the roof. Your soft
green t-shirt. Your
close-cropped beard.
You took me to the racetrack.
You took me to the park.
You said someone should
create The Love Fellowship.
Then being in love
would be all we'd have
to do for a year.
You packed me lunches.
You set up our checking.
You and the mailman,
the woman muttered
walking past
as you sat on the stoop,
reading. *You and the mailman*
have nice legs. In a few years
we'd have our girl in the summer.
You walking her for hours
in a sling down Bergen Avenue,
down Montgomery. But
this summer it was just us,
just you meeting me
halfway on my walk home
from the train. You walking
me there in the morning.

The heat was a thrill, incessant.
There was your hand with its new
ring. Your lips.

What Poems Are

If poems begin
with hand wringing
or flying then
what are poems?

To be a witch,
you have to
feel it.
You have to
leave your head,
put yourself
in someone else's
hands.

What poets have said:
We're all a little bit
necrophiliac.
We're all a little bit
off.

I have read poetry
and studied poems
but I can never
remember what

a poem is

or how to make

a poem.

You collage it

and fake it,

lost in grief

you make it

with black silk.

It's like sewing,

it's like cooking,

it's like painting,

it's like talking.

Poems fan the fire,

are the fire,

hold the water,

vanish in the

steam and smoke.

I've seen them.

They walk

on manly legs

into the world

and then, suddenly,

scale a tree.

Skirts trailing

down.